Mr R S Hawkins
46 Birch Grove
Dunfermline
Fife
KY11 8BE

F.S.

T.T24/
/A.H.34

D0493084

TWILIGHT OF SCOTTISH STEAM

Stanier 'Black Five', No. 45025, stands at St. Margaret's, Edinburgh in 1965. Built by Vulcan Foundry in 1934 this was one of the last of the class to be withdrawn in 1968. In the background stands a Thompson Bl class 4-6-0.

Dr David J. Hucknall

Oxford Publishing Co.

Dedication

To My Parents

A FOULIS-OPC Railway Book

© 1988 Dr. D. J. Hucknall & Haynes Publishing Group

British Library Cataloguing in Publication Data
Hucknall, D.J.
    Twilight of Scottish steam.
    1. Scotland. Steam locomotives, 1962-1967
    I. Title
    625.2'61'09411
    ISBN 0-86093-391-1

Published by:
Haynes Publishing Group
Sparkford, Near Yeovil, Somerset. BA22 7JJ

Haynes Publications Inc.
861 Lawrence Drive, Newbury Park, California 91320. USA.

Frontispiece: Peppercorn Class A2 Pacific, No. 60530 *Sayajirao,* stands under the coaling stage at Dundee Tay Bridge shed in March 1965.

Contents

Acknowledgements

I am extremely grateful to my sister, Sylvia, for suggesting initially that I should publish a selection of my photographs. In this context I should particularly like to thank Mr Philip Hartley and Mr Derek Mercer who were so very helpful and painstaking in printing many difficult negatives.

I also wish to express my thanks to W.A.C. Smith, James L. Stevenson, Hamish Stevenson, John S. Whiteley and Gavin W. Morrison for giving me permission to include some of their superb photographs in this collection. Unless stated otherwise, photographs are by the author.

Finally, I should like to acknowledge the considerable contribution of my wife, Susan, who encouraged me throughout this project.

Left: In the company of a North Eastern Region allocated Class 40, No. D256, Gresley A3 Pacific, No. 60052 *Prince Palatine,* awaits its next turn of duty at St. Margaret's.

A4 Pacific, No. 60007 *Sir Nigel Gresley* basks in the sun at Perth depot in the company of 'Black Five' No. 45473.

6

Introduction

Twenty five years on, it is impossible to define precisely the onset of 'twilight' for the steam locomotive in Scotland. The year 1962 was probably the significant date. Certainly, with the beginning of the summer service of 1962, almost no steam locomotives could be found in the Northern Division of the Scottish Region. According to contemporary railway magazines, in late June 1962 the only steam locomotives on the Highland lines were the shunter at Dingwall and an ex-CR 0-4-4T serving as a stationary boiler in Inverness. The sole occupant of Mallaig shed was a dead BR Standard Class 4 2-6-0 locomotive. Further, in its final withdrawals of 1962, the Scottish Region disposed of 213 locomotives, and the last representatives of classes such as the ex-LNER J35, J39, J83, J88, N15, V1 and Y9 were removed from stock. More importantly, the first withdrawals of 'Coronation' Pacifics and the unfortunate 'Clans' also began. Other classes no longer to be found thereafter in the allocations to Scottish sheds were the 'Jubilees', 'Royal Scots' and Stanier Class 8F 2-8-0s. The last steam engine north of Inverness was removed on 5th December 1962 when the shunter, ex WR No. 1649, left Dingwall.

In spite of this, some superb, distinguished locomotives remained in Scotland. Awful weather in January 1963 brought about the reactivation of several previously-stored A3s, including *Ormonde, Call Boy, Spearmint* and *Papyrus. Salmon Trout* even went to Doncaster for a major overhaul. Further, in 1963, the Glasgow to Aberdeen services were operated with a variety of engines – 'Royal Scots', 'Black Fives' and Als, and rebuilt 'Patriots' and 'Royal Scots' could even be seen at Waverley. Later that year, seven A4s were transferred to Scotland from King's Cross shed via New England motive power depot and, after a period in store, engines such as *Lord Faringdon,* which had, in the 1950s, performed so well on expresses such as "The Elizabethan" and the "Tees-Tyne Pullman", were once again back at work. Also, in 1964/5, the 'Britannia' Pacifics, which had once been so highly regarded at sheds such as Norwich and Stratford, became increasingly common in Scotland on trains from Carlisle.

Within four years, however, night had virtually fallen. Towards the end of 1966, steam was involved in three areas of working – coal trains from Fife, two trains daily in each direction between Glasgow and Fife, and sundry parcels and freight workings to and from Carlisle. By November 1966 however, Buchanan Street Station, Glasgow, had closed, ending the Glasgow to Fife steam workings, and Thornton Junction motive power depot had been dieselised. A Type 2 diesel had taken over the last regular steam working on the Glasgow to Aberdeen line – the 19.00 Perth to Aberdeen. The Scottish Region finally disposed of its allocated steam in early 1967 and, by reorganising locomotive diagrams from Carlisle, the regular use of steam locomotives on Anglo-Scottish trains ended in June of that year. Thereafter, only isolated workings brought steam north of the border.

My own association with locomotives in Scotland began in 1964 when I went to work in Leith. St. Margaret's motive power depot was within walking distance, and shift work gave me the opportunity to visit the shed on very many occasions. St. Margaret's depot was cramped and dirty and overlooked by tenements. It had once had a large complement of undistinguished engines (135 in 1961) but by 1965 the number was 40 and falling rapidly. The entrance to 64A from Clockmill Road consisted of a passage with glass-covered illuminated notice boards on the wall. From the end of this passage, one could look across the lines to the main shed and coaling stage. A lasting memory of 64A is the sound of steam escaping fully from the safety-valves of a V2 and echoing and re-echoing in the wind from the high retaining walls around the shed.

I was also extremely fortunate in being able to visit Perth shed on a number of occasions. Perth always seemed to have unexpected engines. I remember a visit in 1964 particularly. Deep inside the shed was the Stanier Pacific *City of Lancaster.* Incredibly, 36 days later, all the Stanier Pacifics had been withdrawn, some of them in first-class mechanical order. As far as the rest of Scotland was concerned I tried to visit as many sheds as I could as often as I could, and I have included in this album photographs taken in Aberdeen, Bathgate, Dumfries, Dalry Road, etc.

Throughout my time in Scotland, I found that its railwaymen treated me with great tolerance and were remarkably helpful and kind. I hope that I have partly repaid my debt by selecting photographs from my own collection which show these men going about their duties conscientiously in what must have been hopeless circumstances.

Finally, it has given me great pleasure to bring together the photographs for this album. I have tried to assemble the best material available. I have also attempted to avoid the cliché both in word and photograph, hoping to emphasise that the twilight of Scottish steam was made up not only of clean, named locomotives "drifting", "threading" or "coasting", three-quarters on to the camera, on summer days, but also of dirty, undistinguished locomotives, standing about in filthy sheds in Bathgate or Dunfermline, or working trains into Falkirk, for example, on cold and rainy February days.

Although most of the photographs cover the 'twilight' years of 1962 on, I have not been able to resist a handful that were taken rather earlier. I am sure that no one could complain.

The Black Fives

No. 45125 is shown climbing Beattock on a spring Sunday morning in 1962. This locomotive was withdrawn from service later that year.

John S. Whiteley

The majority of locomotives allocated to Perth were 'Black Fives'. A Perth engine for many years, No. 44704 was photographed near the motive power depot on an April evening in 1965.

No. 45489 stands at Perth shed in April 1965.

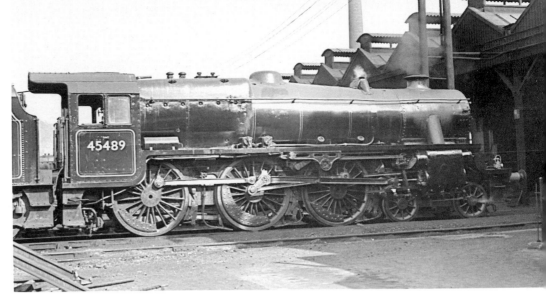

No. 45165 descends Glencruitten Summit towards Oban on 28th July 1961 with the 7.50am Glasgow to Oban train.

John S. Whiteley

No. 44794 leaves Gleneagles with the 'up' "Grampian" on 28th May 1966. This locomotive was withdrawn in April 1967.

John S. Whiteley

Falkirk (Grahamston) on 13th February 1965, and No. 45389 is shown entering the station with the 1.26pm Stirling to Edinburgh (Waverley) train.

W. A. C. Smith

No. 44925 shunts empty stock at Perth Station on the morning of 17th May 1965.

No. 44900 heads a 'down' freight near Lamington, ten miles from Carstairs, on the Carlisle to Carstairs line, 17th July 1965.

James L. Stevenson

No. 45483 is pictured at Dalry Road shed, Edinburgh, on 20th March 1965. Dalry Road closed in October 1965, and No. 45483 was among the engines transferred to St. Margaret's.

No. 45161 moves empty stock from the 8.15am Newcastle to Stranraer Harbour train to Stranraer Town on 31st July 1965.

James L. Stevenson

No. 44704 is seen at Perth motive power depot on 24th April 1965.

Callander on 19th July 1961, and No. 45356 arrives with the 9.30am Oban to Glasgow train.

John S. Whiteley

No. 44986 waits at 63A (Perth shed) on the evening of Sunday, 3rd April 1965.

Near County March Summit, Tyndrum, on 3rd April 1961, No. 44908 heads the 2.12pm Fort William to Glasgow train.

James L. Stevenson

Photographed at Perth depot in 1965, No. 44931 was withdrawn from service at the end of October that year.

No. 45488 of Grangemouth is pictured at its home shed on 4th April 1965. On closure of Grangemouth in October 1965, No. 45488 was transferred to Corkerhill, Glasgow (67A). Note tablet catching apparatus on cab side.

No. 45465 leaves Glasgow (Buchanan Street) with a 5.20pm relief train for Aberdeen on 27th September 1963.

W. A. C. Smith

No. 45471, with a Dumfries (67E) shed plate but with St. Rollox written on the buffer beam, is pictured in early 1965 at Dumfries motive power depot. No. 45471 was withdrawn in July of that year.

No. 45053 stands at Dalry Road shed, Edinburgh, on a bitterly cold day in January 1965.

A Carlisle (Kingmoor) locomotive, No. 44986, stands at Perth depot on 3rd April 1965.

Withdrawn at the end of 1962, No. 45165 was photographed at Pitlochry heading the 10.35am Glasgow to Inverness train towards the Pass of Killiekrankie on 22nd July 1961.

John S. Whiteley

No. 44795 of Carlisle (Kingmoor) was observed at Perth motive power depot, 24th April 1965.

Tenderless, No. 45423 stands at Perth depot in 1965, with 'Patriot' No. 45512 (formerly *Bunsen*) and A4 No. 60006 *Sir Ralph Wedgwood*.

Almost the last steam working in Scotland, Kingmoor engine No. 44672 leaves Glasgow (Central) for Polmadie after having worked the 9.20am from St. Pancras forward from Carlisle on 19th August 1967.

James L. Stevenson

In the type of photograph made famous by the late Bishop Eric Treacy, No. 44908 is shown cruising down Beattock Bank, near Greskine box, with an 'up' fitted freight on 15th April 1963.

John S. Whiteley

No. 45477 stands in the sun at Dalry Road shed, Edinburgh on 13th February 1965.

No. 44899 waits at Glasgow (Central) on 5th April 1967, with the 3.57pm train to Gourock. This locomotive is fitted with a snow plough.
Hamish Stevenson

No. 45261, of Edge Hill depot, Liverpool, is pictured receiving attention at St. Margaret's on 27th March 1965.

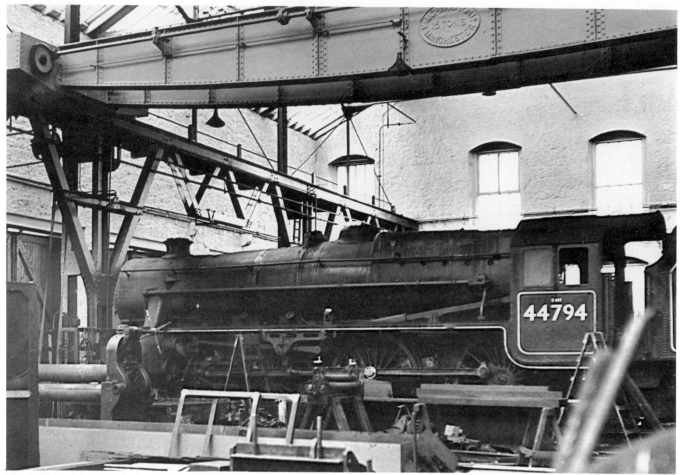

No. 44794, withdrawn in late April 1967, undergoes repairs at Inverurie Works on 25th April 1965.

No. 45474 is seen on the turntable at Ferryhill shed, Aberdeen, on 6th March 1965. The locomotive was withdrawn in Autumn 1966.

Leaving Paisley (Gilmour Street) on 13th April 1967, No. 44911 heads the 5.20pm from Glasgow to Gourock.

James L. Stevenson

The 5.33pm train from St. Enoch to East Kilbride leaves Busby (a few miles to the south-west of Glasgow) headed by No. 45363 of Carlisle (Kingmoor), on 12th April 1965.

W.A.C. Smith

Running approximately parallel to Salamander Street in Leith was a goods line serving various factories. In this photograph No. 44702, of Dalry Road, is seen shunting outside the premises of Scottish Agricultural Industries Ltd on 21st January 1965.

The A1s, A2s and A3s

The great majority of Scottish A1s, A2s and A3s were associated with Haymarket shed, Edinburgh. Over a period of about three years (1960–63), these locomotives were removed and either stored or transferred to St. Margaret's. The A1s (Nos 60152/59/60-62), for example, were sent to 64A in October 1963, and they had certainly disappeared by mid-1964. Of the formerly-large allocation of A3s, only *Salmon Trout* and *Spearmint* survived to the beginning of 1965. The A2s fared little better – *Hornet's Beauty* lasted until June 1965, although *Sayajirao* was not withdrawn until the end of 1966.

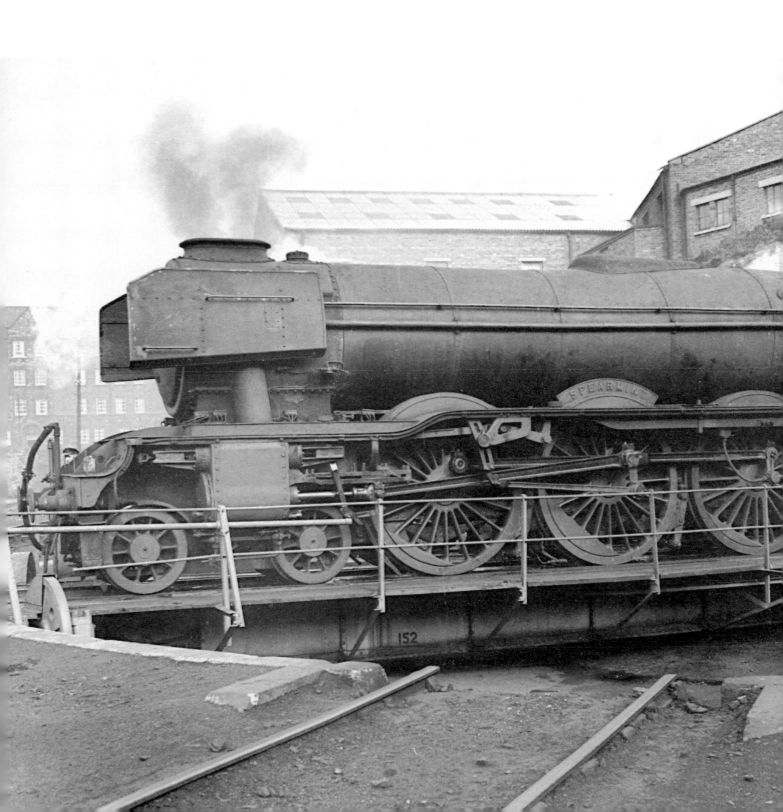

Previous page and above: A3 4-6-2 No. 60100 *Spearmint,* is pictured on the turntable at St. Margaret's shed on 17th April 1965. Whilst allocated to Haymarket, No. 60100 had been the engine assigned to driver Norman McKillop and had been the subject of several articles published in *Trains Illustrated* in the 1950s. *Spearmint* was withdrawn in June 1965.

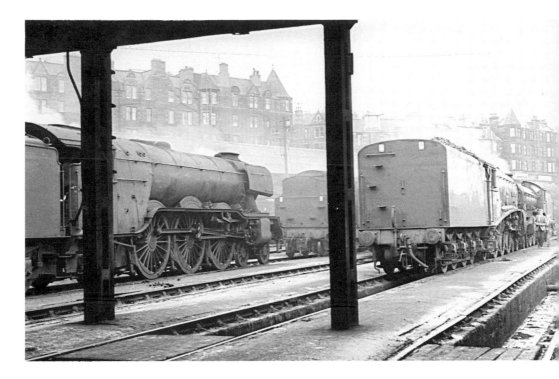

Above and below: No. 60100 *Spearmint,* again photographed at St. Margaret's in April 1965.

A3 No. 60099 *Call Boy* had been one of Haymarket's large allocation of A3s. It was transferred to St. Margaret's at the very end of 1962 and in this photograph it is seen preparing to leave Waverley with the 'up' "Anglo-Scottish Car Carrier" on 17th July 1961.

John S. Whiteley

A3 4-6-2 No. 60052 *Prince Palatine* was transferred from Gateshead to St. Margaret's in June 1963. In this photograph it is seen leaving Edinburgh (Waverley) on 19th June 1965 with a train for Carlisle.

A3 class No. 60080 *Dick Turpin*, of Holbeck depot, Leeds and BR Standard Class 5 4-6-2 No. 73101, head the 6.38pm car sleeper from Glasgow (St. Enoch) to London (Marylebone). The pair were photographed on the Kilmarnock line, near Dunlop on 24th July 1963.

W.A.C. Smith

Peppercorn A2 4-6-2 No. 60530 *Sayajirao* is pictured under the coaling stage at Dundee (Tay Bridge) at 12.50pm on 6th March 1965. It was withdrawn from service in October/November 1966.

No. 60530 *Sayajirao* at St. Margaret's shed, Edinburgh in June 1965.

Peppercorn A2 4-6-2 No. 60534 *Irish Elegance* approaches Edinburgh (Waverley) through Princes Street Gardens with a fitted freight on 17th July 1961.   *John S. Whiteley*

A2 class No. 60512 (formerly *Steady Aim*) is seen at Perth depot on the evening of 27th June 1965. No. 60512 had been transferred from York in 1962, initially to Edinburgh and later to Polmadie, Glasgow. It remained at Perth certainly until September 1965.

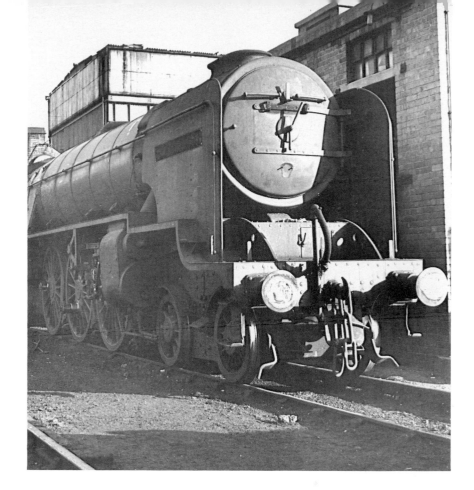

A2 4-6-2 No. 60527 *Sun Chariot* of Polmadie, Glasgow stands at Aberdeen Station on Saturday, 28th March 1964.

Gavin W. Morrison

Al Pacifics were unusual on the West Coast Main Line but No. 60118 *Archibald Sturrock* was photographed passing Lamington, ten miles from Carstairs on the Carstairs to Carlisle line, southbound, on 1st August 1964 with an empty stock train.

James L. Stevenson

A1 4-6-2 No. 60147 *North Eastern* of York depot is seen at Corstorphine on 30th April 1964 with the 2.42pm train to Edinburgh. The engine and train would have then worked the 3.48pm local to Berwick on Tweed.

James L. Stevenson

Seen at Carlisle (Kingmoor) on 21st March 1965, A1 Pacific No. 60131 *Osprey* had been heading an RCTS Leeds to Carlisle railtour. *Osprey* was withdrawn seven months later.

The A4s

Several A4s were always allocated to Haymarket motive power depot in Edinburgh, usually for use on expresses to King's Cross out of Waverley Station. During 1962 however, these engines were transferred to other depots. *William Whitelaw* (60004), *Union of South Africa* (60009), *Empire of India* (60011) and *Kingfisher* (60024) were transferred to Ferryhill whilst *Commonwealth of Australia* (60012), *Merlin* (60027) and *Golden Plover* (60031) went to St. Rollox. With the possible exception of *Empire of India* (60011), which was withdrawn in the first half of 1964, all survived at least until the end of 1965.

With the inauguration of the summer timetable in 1963, steam was forbidden on the East Coast Main Line south of Peterborough. Several A4s which had been until then associated with King's Cross depot went eventually to Scotland. Engines such as *Sir Ralph Wedgwood* (60006), *Sir Nigel Gresley* (60007), *Dominion of Canada* (60010), *Silver King* (60016), *Golden Eagle* (60023), *Miles Beevor* (60026) and *Lord Faringdon* (60034) were transferred to Aberdeen and could often be seen at Perth or St. Margaret's up to about mid-1965 (for the record, however, No. 60023 was being dismantled at Ferryhill by March 1965). Thereafter, fewer and fewer survived.

Non-stop expresses between King's Cross and Edinburgh, such as "The Elizabethan", were some of the hardest tasks set to British passenger locomotives. Running demanded hard steaming for more than six hours without a break, and the engines allocated to such duties were specially selected and in the best condition. This photograph, taken on 17th July 1961, shows A4 4-6-2 No. 60028 *Walter K. Whigham* of King's Cross, leaving Edinburgh for London.

John S. Whiteley

On 18th July 1961, the 'up' "Elizabethan" was hauled by Haymarket A4 class No. 60024 *Kingfisher*.

John S. Whiteley

On 8th June 1965, the 'up' "Grampian" was hauled by No. 60009 *Union of South Africa*.

John S. Whiteley

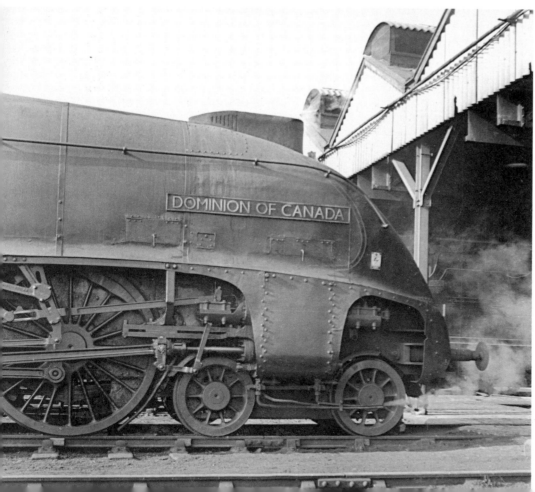

Above and left: On 6th March 1965, No. 60010 *Dominion of Canada* of Ferryhill shed was photographed outside the southern end of Perth depot. No. 60010 had been sent from New England motive power depot at the end of October 1963. At this time it appeared to be in good external condition and yet it was withdrawn only three months later. It was taken to Darlington for demolition and the task had already started when Canadian interests ensured preservation of the locomotive in that country.

No. 60027 *Merlin* is seen waiting with other engines at the coaling stage at St. Margaret's depot, Edinburgh in early 1965. *Merlin* was withdrawn in the early autumn of that year. Earlier, in February 1962, No. 60027 was the engine selected for trials on the Glasgow to Aberdeen three-hour schedule.

A small boy turns his back on No. 60019 *Bittern* at Perth depot on 16th August 1964.

No. 60019 *Bittern* is shown leaving Perth Station with the 'down' "St. Mungo" on 20th April 1965.

Almost at the end of its working life, No. 60019 *Bittern* was photographed leaving Perth with the 'up' "Granite City" on 27th May 1966. On 3rd September 1966 it headed a special train run by the Scottish Region, but was withdrawn shortly afterwards.

John S. Whiteley

Standing in the rain at St. Margaret's shed in February 1965, No. 60006 *Sir Ralph Wedgwood* was photographed with V2 2-6-2 No. 60813 and A3 4-6-2 No. 60100 *Spearmint*.

No. 60006 *Sir Ralph Wedgwood* leaves Perth Station on 20th April 1965 with the combination of the 'up' TPO and the 5.10pm Perth to Carstairs.

John S. Whiteley

No. 60034 *Lord Faringdon*, once used on expresses such as "The Elizabethan", enters Buchanan Street Station, Glasgow with a football special from Aberdeen on 26th March 1966. No. 60034 was withdrawn in August 1966.

James L. Stevenson

No. 60034 *Lord Faringdon* was sent from New England to the Scottish Region at the end of October 1963. It was then stored at Bathgate until mid-May 1964 when it was reactivated. In this view No. 60034 is seen on 24th August 1964, arriving at Stirling with the 'up' TPO.

John S. Whiteley

No. 60007 *Sir Nigel Gresley,* of Ferryhill depot, Aberdeen, is seen leaving Perth with the 'up' "Bon Accord" on 24th August 1965
John S. Whiteley

No. 60007 *Sir Nigel Gresley* photographed at St. Margaret's in the summer of 1965.

No. 60007 *Sir Nigel Gresley* at St. Margaret's depot in 1964. Sent to the Scottish Region at the end of October 1963, No. 60007 was stored for six months at Dalry Road. It was then transferred to Ferryhill to work the Aberdeen to Glasgow service.

No. 60026 *Miles Beevor* is pictured at St. Margaret's on 13th March 1965. After seven months in store at Bathgate, No. 60026 was transferred to Aberdeen, Ferryhill, in May 1964. It was finally withdrawn around December 1965.

One of the few photographs of No. 60016 *Silver King* in her days in Scotland. The locomotive is seen at Perth shed on 2nd April 1965. No. 60016 was withdrawn and condemned about this time, after having sustained damage to her middle cylinder and motion in an accident at Glamis. It was said that the engine sent to recover *Silver King* collided heavily with it and worsened the situation.

Both these photographs show No. 60006 *Sir Ralph Wedgwood* on shed. Below, the engine is at St. Margaret's in 1965 whilst left, it is seen at Perth depot on 16th August 1964.

No. 60002 *Sir Murrough Wilson* passes through Duddingston and Craigmillar Station on 8th September 1962 with a freight for Millerhill Yard. In the station stands a Gloucester two-car diesel multiple unit on the last day of the passenger service on the Edinburgh Outer Circle line.

James L. Stevenson

No. 60024 *Kingfisher* is seen at 63A (Perth) in 1965. This locomotive was responsible for the last A4 working out of Aberdeen in September 1966.

The BR Standard Locomotives

British Railways Standard locomotives, such as the Class 5MT 4-6-0s, the Class 4, 3 and 2MT 2-6-0s and the Class 4 2-6-4Ts, were always well represented in Scotland. Further, of the Pacifics, the 'Clans' were at one time all allocated to either Polmadie or Kingmoor sheds and a handful of 'Britannias', *(Firth of Clyde, Firth of Forth,* etc.) could be found at Polmadie. Between mid-1964 and the beginning of 1965, however, many of the twenty three well-liked Class 7 'Britannia' 4-6-2s, which had worked expresses in and out of Liverpool Street Station in the 1950s, were sent to Carlisle (Kingmoor) shed, where they hauled trains to and from Scotland.

Class 7 'Britannia' Pacific No. 70005 (formerly *John Milton)* leaves Stirling on 21st April 1965 with a parcels train for Perth.
John S. Whiteley

'Britannia' Pacific No. 70037 *Hereward the Wake* is pictured at Perth shed on 7th March 1965.

'Britannia' 4-6-2 No. 70007 (formerly *Coeur de Lion*) is seen at Perth shed on 2nd April 1965.

St. Enoch Station, Glasgow on 5th May 1964 and Class 7 'Britannia' No. 70039 *Sir Christopher Wren* is seen heading the 5.30pm train to Carlisle, whilst Class 4 2-6-4T No. 80058 stands with the 5.33pm train to East Kilbride.

W.A.C Smith

At Perth shed in June 1965, 'Black Five' No. 44900 (12A) casts a shadow on 'Britannia' Class No. 70005 (formerly *John Milton*).

'Britannia' 4-6-2s No. 70036 (formerly *Boadicea)* and No. 70008 (formerly *Black Prince)* stand outside Perth shed in 1965.

On 24th August 1964, at Dunblane Station, 'Britannia' No. 70035 *Rudyard Kipling* heads the 9.25am Crewe to Perth and Aberdeen working.

John S. Whiteley

Class 7 'Britannia' No. 70031 (formerly *Byron*) stands at Perth Station on 8th June 1965 with the 4.47pm. 'up' fish train.

John S. Whiteley

Glasgow (Central), on 15th July 1967 and 'Britannia' 4-6-2 No. 70028 (formerly *Royal Star*) proceeds to Polmadie depot after working the 6.40am from Birmingham forward from Carlisle. The locomotive was withdrawn during that September/October.

James L. Stevenson

Previously of Cardiff (Canton) and Trafford Park depots, 'Britannia' No. 70021 (formerly *Morning Star*) takes water at New Cumnock on 22nd July 1967.

James L. Stevenson

Class 6 'Clan' Pacific No. 72001 *Clan Cameron* is pictured at Greskine on 24th April 1962.

John S. Whiteley

Wandelmill, about three miles from Abington, on 14th July 1962 and *Clan Cameron* heads the 8.07am Glasgow to Morecambe train.

James L. Stevenson

'Clan' Pacific No. 72007 *Clan Macintosh* stands at Stirling on 24th August 1964 with an afternoon 'up' fish train.

John S. Whiteley

BR Standard Class 5 4-6-0 No. 73077 and B1 Class 4-6-0 No. 61140 cross Fillan Viaduct at Crianlarich, heading the 2.12pm Fort William to Glasgow train, on 8th August 1959. The mountain in the background is Ben More (3,843ft.).

James L. Stevenson

BR Standard Class 5 4-6-0 No. 73124 descends Beattock Bank on 15th April 1964 with an 'up' mixed freight.

John S. Whiteley

BR Standard Class 5 4-6-0 No. 73149 of St. Rollox depot (65B) and 'Black Five' No. 44722 of Perth (63A), stand at Perth shed on the evening of 27th June 1965.

BR Standard Class 5 4-6-0 No. 73056 leaves Stirling with the 3.30pm Aberdeen to Glasgow train on 21st April 1965.

John S. Whiteley

Perth motive power depot on 3rd April 1965, and BR Standard 4-6-0 No. 73145, fitted with a snowplough in spite of the fact that winter was well over, stands with 'Britannia' Pacific No. 70007 (formerly *Coeur de Lion*).

A pair of BR Standard Class 5 4-6-0s, Nos 73147 and 73008, are seen at Perth shed on 7th March 1965.

Gleneagles on 21st August 1964 and **BR** Standard Class 5 4-6-0 No. 73151 heads the 4.14pm Edinburgh to Perth train.

John S. Whiteley

BR Standard Class 4 2-6-4T No. 80052 and Class 5 4-6-0 No. 73122 are seen at Kilmacolm on 6th July 1963, with the 9.53am "Orange Walk" special from Glasgow (St. Enoch) to Lynedoch.

W.A.C. Smith

Perth Station on 24th August 1964, where BR Standard Class 5 4-6-0 No. 73146 of St. Rollox shed was photographed heading the 10.00am Dundee to Glasgow express.

John S. Whiteley

BR Standard Class 5 4-6-0 No. 73099 awaits attention at Inverurie Works, Aberdeenshire, on 25th April 1965.

Ibrox Station on 22nd August 1962 with BR Standard Class 4 2-6-0 No. 76001 heading a football special from Springburn, whilst Class 4 2-6-4T No. 80109 passes with the 7.05pm Glasgow Central to Gourock train.

W.A.C. Smith

BR Standard Class 4 2-6-0 No. 76111, formerly of Thornton and Dunfermline depots, is seen at Bathgate at noon on 4th April 1965.

Class 9F 2-10-0 No. 92099, fitted with Westinghouse brake gear, is pictured at Kingmoor shed, Carlisle, on 21st March 1965. Kingmoor received an allocation of 9Fs in mid-1964 in order to work Shap to Ravenscraig limestone trains.

Class 9F 2-10-0 No. 92233, formerly of Cardiff (Canton) heads a 'down' freight near Lamington on 16th July 1965.

James L. Stevenson

Photographed between Busby and Thorntonhall on 25th June 1964, Class 4 2-6-4T No. 80046 heads the 5.08pm Glasgow (St. Enoch) to East Kilbride train.

W.A.C. Smith

Class 4 2-6-4T No. 80124 waits at Dundee with the 12.28pm train to Tayport on 8th February 1964.

James L. Stevenson

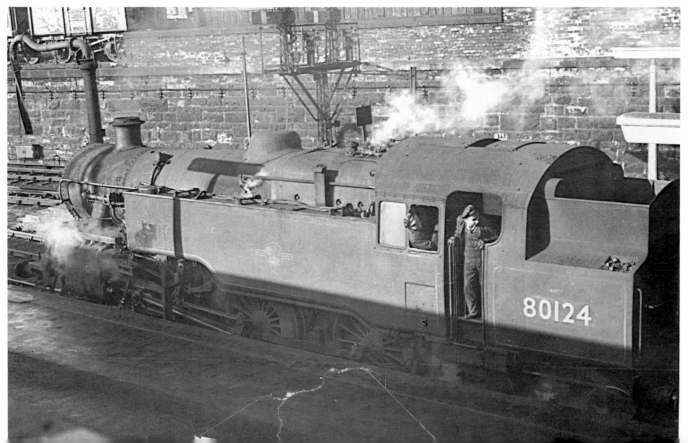

A line of Class 4 2-6-4Ts wait for coal at St. Margaret's shed, Edinburgh on 20th March 1965.

'Black Five' 4-6-0 No. 44672 and BR Class 4 2-6-4T No. 80119 are seen at Dumfries shed in March 1965.

Class 4 2-6-4T No. 80117 stands at New Galloway with the 8am Stranraer Town to Dumfries train on 11th June 1965. This line was closed three days later.

James L. Stevenson

Class 4 2-6-4T No. 80114 and ex-LNER B1 4-6-0 No. 61324 stand at St. Margaret's shed (64A) in 1965.

Class 2 2-6-0 No. 78050, formerly of Motherwell, is shown at Bathgate on 4th April 1965.

On 27th March 1965, at St. Margaret's shed a boisterous wind was blowing smoke and steam away from V2 Class 2-6-2 No. 60836. Apart from a short time at Eastfield shed in 1960, No. 60836 was always a 64A engine. Clayton Class 17 diesel electric No. D8576 is on the left.

The V2 2-6-2s

One hundred and eighty four Gresley-designed locomotives made up the Class V2. Of these, approximately forty engines were allocated to Scottish sheds such as Dundee, Aberdeen (Ferryhill) and the Edinburgh sheds of Haymarket and St. Margaret's. The following photographs shows several members of this pleasant group of locomotives at various locations in Scotland.

No. 60824 stands in the dirt of St. Margaret's shed on a rainy day in March 1965.

No. 60824 photographed in better conditions, again at St. Margaret's.

No. 60919 (left) enters Stirling Station on 27th September 1965 with the 2pm Dundee to Glasgow (Buchanan St.) express. Stirling 'Black Five' No. 45359 waits in the bay platform with the 3.40pm train for Falkirk and Edinburgh.

W.A.C. Smith

Ferryhill, Aberdeen on 21st July 1961 and No. 60824 passes with a southbound fish train. This locomotive was relatively long-lived, surviving until almost the end of 1966.
John S. Whiteley

No. 60955, of Ferryhill shed, is seen at St. Margaret's on 20th March 1965.

No. 60840 (64A) approaches Whitrope Summit (915ft.) in the Cheviots, with a 'down' freight on Saturday, 8th July 1961. The ex-North British main line (the Waverley Route) northwards from Carlisle was the most difficult of the express routes taken by Anglo-Scottish traffic.

Gavin W. Morrison

No. 60919 stands at St. Margaret's shed waiting for coal on 27th March 1965.

A close-up view of a V2 taken at St. Margaret's depot in 1965.

No. 60835 *The Green Howard, Alexandra, Princess of Wales's Own Yorkshire Regiment* (a name rivalling that of No. 60809 in length), is seen on an 'up' local train at Hawick on 8th July 1961.

Gavin W. Morrison

No. 60931 undergoes smokebox cleaning at its home shed on 17th April 1965.

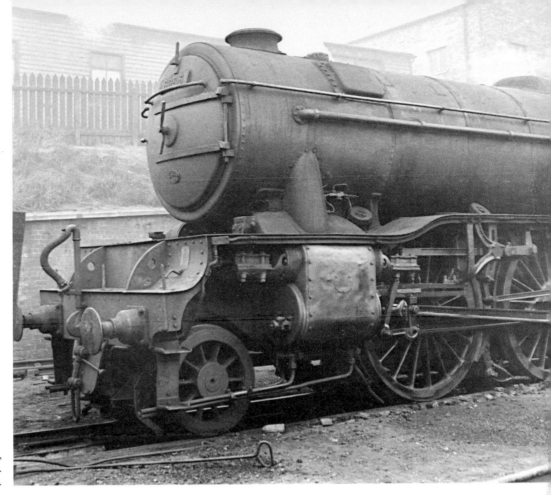

Two views of No. 60816 (64A), photographed on 13th March 1965. It was withdrawn seven months later.

No. 60970 (on the left) stands with No. 60931 in the shed yard at St. Margaret's on 14th February 1965.

No. 60931 showers St. Margaret's shed with steam and water in early 1965. The locomotive was withdrawn in September of that year.

Sun shining through the roof of St. Margaret's shed illuminates the dome of a V2 on 20th March 1965.

A pair of V2s at St. Margaret's, with No. 60919, right.

'Jubilee' Class 4-6-0 No. 45573 *Newfoundland* is seen at Kingmoor on 21st March 1965.

The Stanier 6Ps, 7Ps and 8Ps

Some 'Jubilee', 'Royal Scot' and 'Coronation' class locomotives had a long association with certain Scottish sheds, many of them being based at the same depot for several years. For example, the 'Jubilees' *Madras* and *Bombay* were among Corkerhill's allocation of locomotives in 1937, and remained there probably until the early 1950s when they were sent to England. Similarly, *Assam* and *North West Frontier* remained at Polmadie for more than thirteen years.

Larger Stanier locomotives tended to be kept at Polmadie for working Anglo-Scottish expresses, and a group of 'Royal Scots' (Nos 46102, 46104, 46105, 46107 and 46121) and 'Coronations' (Nos 46222, 46223, 46224, 46227, 46230, 46231 and 46232) remained there until their withdrawal. In April 1961 however, Carlisle (Kingmoor) received an allocation of the latter (Nos 46221, 46226, 46237, 46244, 46252, 46255 and 46257) and they were used regularly on short trips to places such as Kilmarnock and Glasgow (St. Enoch). Latterly, Kingmoor also received both 'Royal Scots' and some rebuilt 'Patriots' but their activities were relatively short-lived.

Dirty and forgotten, 'Jubilee' 4-6-0 No. 45588 (formerly *Kashmir*) stands at Kingmoor in March 1965.

Near Sanquhar on 12th August 1961, 'Jubilee' No. 45564 *New South Wales* heads a 'down' train. Almost exactly three years later, No. 45564 was withdrawn from service.

James L. Stevenson

'Jubilee' No. 45653 *Barham,* photographed between Beattock Summit and Elvanfoot on 14th July 1962, heads the 8.50am Blackpool to Glasgow express.

James L. Stevenson

No. 45602 *British Honduras* climbs Beattock near Harthope with a morning Liverpool to Glasgow train, on 23rd April 1962.

John S. Whiteley

'Jubilee' 4-6-0 No. 45717 *Dauntless,* photographed near Abington on 15th July 1961, hauls the 10.50am Glasgow (Central) to Liverpool train.

James L. Stevenson

No. 45717 *Dauntless* of Bank Hall shed, helped at the rear by a 2-6-4T, heads the 9.43am Liverpool to Glasgow express up Beattock Bank on 21st April 1962.

John S. Whiteley

Near Kirkconnel, on 12th August 1961, 'Jubilee' No. 45692 *Cyclops* heads a Glasgow (St. Enoch) to Leeds train. Formerly of Crewe, Polmadie and Perth, *Cyclops* would have been allocated to Corkerhill shed when this photograph was taken. Latterly, the Scottish 'Jubilees' were poorly kept and by the end of 1962 the Region rid itself of these delightful engines.

James L. Stevenson

No. 45613 *Kenya* heads the 10.15am Edinburgh to Birmingham train near Abington on 15th July 1961.

James L. Stevenson

Detail of 'Jubilee' No. 45629 *Straits Settlements* at Perth in August 1964. During its lifetime No. 45629 was allocated to many sheds including Derby (1937), Bristol (1942), Trafford Park (1948), Longsight (1958) and Crewe North (1959-62) before its final transfer to Kingmoor.

By coincidence 'Patriot' 6P 4-6-0 No. 45517 was photographed heading the 9.30am relief from Southport to Glasgow at two locations on 29th July 1961. Above the train is on Beattock Bank and below, near Symington.

W.A.C. Smith/James L. Stevenson

'Patriot' 7P 4-6-0 (an Ivatt rebuild) No. 45512 (formerly *Bunsen*) takes water at Dumfries on 21st March 1965, whilst heading a Carlisle to Glasgow parcels train. *Bunsen* and *Sir Frederick Harrison* (No. 45531) were both allocated to Kingmoor and were by then the sole survivors of the class.

Passing Lamington on 1st August 1964, 'Royal Scot' 7P No. 46128 *The Lovat Scouts* was photographed on an 'up' train.

James L. Stevenson

No. 46107 *Argyll and Sutherland Highlander* climbs Beattock at Harthope on 23rd April 1962 with the 9.30am Manchester to Glasgow express. No. 46107 was scrapped during the following December.

John S. Whiteley

'Royal Scot' 7P No. 46132 (formerly *The King's Regiment, Liverpool*) awaits scrapping at Kingmoor in 1965.

Near Symington on 29th July 1961, No. 46166 *London Rifle Brigade* heads an 'up' train.

James L. Stevenson

No. 46152, *The King's Dragoon Guardsman* is seen at Perth on 6th March 1965. The locomotive was scrapped one month later.

Another photograph of No. 46152. This locomotive was the original No. 6100 *Royal Scot* until 1933 when the two locomotives exchanged identities. The other locomotive was exhibited at the Chicago Century of Progress Exhibition, USA, then being the latest off the production line.

'Coronation' 4-6-2 No. 46247 *City of Liverpool* is shown on Beattock Bank at Harthope, with the 9.50am Euston to Perth express on 23rd April 1962.

John S. Whiteley

'Coronation' Pacific No. 46248 *City of Leeds* leaves Beattock Station with a Birmingham to Glasgow train on 20th May 1961.

Gavin W. Morrison

A Kingmoor-allocated 'Coronation', No. 46244 *King George VI,* passes Harthope with the 9.20am Crewe to Perth working on 23rd April 1962.

John S. Whiteley

No. 46252 *City of Leicester,* of Carlisle (Kingmoor), leaves Beattock Station with a 'down' Euston to Perth train on Saturday, 20th May 1961.

Gavin W. Morrison

At Crawford on 15th April 1963, Crewe North 'Coronation' No. 46256 *Sir William A. Stanier, F.R.S.* heads the 9am Perth to Euston express.

John S. Whiteley

No. 46225 *Duchess of Gloucester* is seen near Lamington with the 10.17am Aberdeen to Euston express on 1st August 1964. No. 46225 was later cut up at the West of Scotland Shipbuilding Co. Ltd.'s yard in Troon.

James L. Stevenson

At Greskine, on the ten-mile climb from Beattock Station to the summit, No. 46249 *City of Sheffield* is shown hauling a Saturday extra, on 14th July 1962.

Gavin W. Morrison

The B1s

Four hundred and ten of Edward Thompson's B1 Class 4-6-0s were built from 1942 to 1952. These locomotives had two outside cylinders, cast from the same patterns as Gresley's Class K2, and the same 6ft 2in driving wheels as the V2 2-6-2s. The B1s were highly regarded, and said to be the equal of the 'Black Fives'.

Approximately seventy five of these locomotives were allocated to Scottish sheds, including Glasgow (Eastfield), Kittybrewster, Dundee, Dalry Road, etc., and several survived until the end of steam traction on the Region.

Sunlight dapples No. 61345 as it stands at St. Margaret's shed. The photograph was taken on the afternoon of 1st May 1965. The engine was withdrawn in August 1966.

No. 61324 moves slowly into the shed yard at St. Margaret's in 1965.

Steam and smoke are blown away from B1 No. 61307, of Dalry Road shed, when photographed in early 1965.

No. 61172 passes Anstruther with the 4.08pm St. Andrews to Glasgow (Queen Street) train, while No. 61140 waits to work the 5.48pm train to Thornton on 21st July 1962.

W.A.C. Smith

Crossing Largo Viaduct on 25th July 1964, No. 61116 is seen hauling the 12.17pm Thornton Junction to Crail working. No. 61116 was withdrawn in August 1966.

W.A.C. Smith

Withdrawn two months later, No. 61278 heads the 10.10am Dundee to Newport-on-Tay (West) freight near its destination, on 16th March 1967.

Hamish Stevenson

No. 61133 leaves Thornton Junction with the 12.30pm Crail to Edinburgh train on 14th August 1965.

W.A.C. Smith

The rapid dieselisation of train services in Edinburgh is apparent in this photograph of No. 61262 leaving the east end of Waverley Station on 23rd July 1962 with empty stock for Craigentinny. To the immediate right of the B1's exhaust, Class 45 'Peak' No. D24 waits with the 'up' "Waverley" whilst on the far right, a 'Deltic' stands with the 'up' "Flying Scotman".

John S. Whiteley

B1s photographed at Dumfermline shed on the evening of Sunday, 4th April 1965.

An ex-LNER B1 and a BR Standard 4MT 2-6-4 No. 80054, are seen inside St. Margaret's shed on 13th March 1965.

No. 61191 acts as station pilot at Edinburgh (Waverley) on 8th May 1965. The locomotive was withdrawn at the end of the following August.

The smokebox detail and nameplate of No. 61245 *Murray of Elibank*, photographed at Dalry Road shed, Edinburgh on 31st January 1965. No. 61245 was withdrawn in the summer of that year.

Dundee-allocated B1 No. 61180 stands at St. Margaret's depot on 13th June 1965. As 1965 progressed, fewer and fewer engines were to be seen at this location.

No. 61396 on shed, in 1965.

The J36s, J37s and J38s

Even up to the mid-1960s, a significant number of these locomotives were active in eastern and central Scotland. The Holmes J36s were almost eighty years old by then, having been introduced by the North British Railway in 1888.

Designed by W.P. Reid and introduced in 1914, the J37s were the final development of the North British Railway goods locomotive, and as late as 1965, these locomotives were still being overhauled at Inverurie Works.

The J38s were relative newcomers to Scotland. Gresley-designed and introduced in 1926, the whole class was allocated to Scottish sheds.

Thornton shed on 24th April 1965, where J38 0-6-0 No. 65922 is seen silhouetted against a threatening sky.

J38 class 0-6-0 No. 65932, pictured at Thornton on 24th April 1965.

St. Margaret's shed on 13th March 1965 and a J38 and an A4 Pacific stand in the yard.

J38 No. 65912 shunts at Salamander Street, Leith, on a frosty day in January 1965.

Ex NBR J36 0-6-0 No. 65234 on the Woodend Colliery branch on 11th June 1963.

W.A.C. Smith

No. 65234 again, at Waverley Station, Edinburgh on 29th August 1964.

J36 Class No. 65297 stands outside the main shed at St. Margaret's on 13th March 1965.

J36 No. 65258 climbs to Dalmeny with the afternoon freight on the South Queensferry branch on 15th August 1961.

W.A.C. Smith

A J37 0-6-0 No. 64621, propels a brake van across the swing bridge over the Forth and Clyde Canal at Orchardhall, on the goods line from Falkirk to Grangemouth, 12th September 1963.

W.A.C. Smith

At Auchterhouse, near Dundee on Saturday 28th March 1964, J37 No. 64618 prepares to leave with an RCTS special.

Gavin W. Morrison

J37 No. 64580 awaits scrapping outside Grangemouth shed on 4th April 1965.

Fresh from Inverurie Works, J37 No. 64569 stands in the shed yard at Aberdeen (Ferryhill) on the afternoon of 6th March 1965.

J37 No. 64620, complete with snowplough is seen inside the shed at Dundee (Tay Bridge).

J37s and other locomotives are pictured at Grangemouth motive power depot in early 1965.

Passing what had been Stannergate Station, J37 No. 64602 heads the 11.18am Dundee to Montrose freight on 26th January 1967.

Hamish Stevenson

J37 No. 64610 stands at Grangemouth depot.

J37 No. 64602 acts as pilot in Dundee (Tay Bridge) yard on 16th March 1967.

Hamish Stevenson

Class J36 No. 65234, heading an SLS special to Leith (Citadel) and Penicuik, is shown at Waverley Station on 29th August 1964. On 7th February 1965 No. 65234 was converted to a stationary boiler at St. Margaret's.

J37 No. 64621, of Grangemouth (65F), is seen in 1965.

Built in 1913 and restored to the livery of the North British Railway Co., No. 256 *Glen Douglas* and J37 No. 64624 approach Jedburgh with an RCTS special on 9th July 1961.
Gavin W. Morrison

One of St. Margaret's many unremarkable engines, Class J38 No. 65929 (fitted with a snowplough) stands at the coaling stage on 13th March 1965.

Thornton shed on 24th April 1965 sees Holmes J36 No. 65287 modified with cut-down boiler mountings and an ugly shortened chimney.

J37 No. 64576 shunts at Dundee (Tay Bridge) in March 1965.

Steam Miscellany

Hughes/Fowler Class 5P4F 2-6-0 No. 42908 of Ayr shed, stands at Inverurie Works in April 1965. Two hundred and forty five of these locomotives were built between 1926 and 1930, and several were allocated to depots such as Ardrossan, Ayr and Hurlford.

Hughes/Fowler 2-6-0 No. 42803 heads a 'down' express freight in the Nith Valley near Sanquhar on 27th July 1963.

W.A.C. Smith

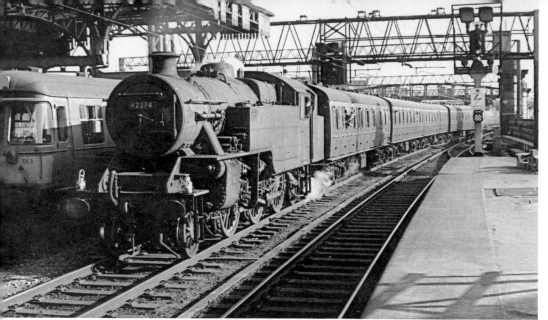

Class 4 2-6-4T No. 42274 was an example of Fairburn's development of a Stanier design. In this photograph the locomotive is shown entering Glasgow (Central) Station with the 5.03pm train from Gourock, on 28th April 1967.

James L. Stevenson

Fairburn Class 4 No. 42273 heads the 11.10am Stirling to Callander train from Bridge of Allan in April 1965.

John S. Whiteley

Aberfeldy, on Saturday 13th June 1959, where the branch line train waits to return to Ballinluig Junction, headed by ex Caledonian Railway McIntosh Class 2P 0-4-4T No. 55218.

Gavin W. Morrison

McIntosh, Caledonian 439 or Standard Passenger class No. 55204 is pictured at Oban on 27th July 1961.

John S. Whiteley

Grangemouth WD Class 2-10-0 No. 90773 stands in Seafield Yard, Leith, on Saturday, 25th August 1961. These locomotives were purchased by British Railways in 1948 from the Ministry of Supply and the majority were allocated to either Grangemouth or Motherwell.

Gavin W. Morrison

British Railways also acquired the smaller WD Class 8F 2-8-0 locomotives from the Ministry of Supply. Here, No. 90444, for several years a Dundee (Tay Bridge) engine, stands under the coaling tower at Thornton shed on 24th April 1965.

Photographed at the south western end of Dunfermline depot in March 1965, WD 2-8-0 No. 90229 awaits its next duty, together with B1 4-6-0 No. 61407.

Out of a class of 128 engines, very few Ivatt Class 2 2-6-0 locomotives had been assigned to Scottish sheds. No. 46462, however, had been at St. Margaret's for several years and is shown at its home shed in mid-March 1965.

A crew member of Ivatt Class 2 No. 46479 greets the crew of 'Black Five' No. 44707 at Gatehouse-of-Fleet on 1st June 1965. No. 46479 had been allocated to Darlington and Heaton sheds in the north east of England before being transferred to Beattock, sometime in 1962.

Hamish Stevenson

Class 3F 0-6-0T No. 47667 is seen at Kingmoor in 1965, equipped with a vacuum brake. Here it was used for the steam-heating of passenger coaches. Over 300 of these locomotives were built but, of these, less than ten were in Scotland. Corkerhill, Polmadie and Hamilton had one or two examples.

A fitting end to the sections on steam locomotives – signals at Seafield (right) and near Ballater (below, right). Photographed in 1965.

The Diesels Take Over

The introduction of diesels to the Scottish Region began fairly early. In late 1959, for example, Type 2s worked on the Glasgow to Mallaig passenger service and also on freights between Perth and Inverness. Oil tanks had been set up at Haymarket motive power depot by March 1960, and the Scottish Region had been loaned some English Electric Type 4s by York shed.

In June 1961, Haymarket's 'Deltics' began regularly to work the 11.00am Edinburgh to King's Cross train as far as Newcastle, and the 11.00am King's Cross to Glasgow express back again. Its Pacifics were left with only three regular passenger duties to and from Newcastle, although they occasionally worked to Carlisle and back with freights. Late in 1961, the 'Deltics' began to haul the morning "Talisman" 'up' to King's Cross, returning with the "Aberdonian".

About the same time, all passenger work on the Perth to Inverness line was handled exclusively by BR/Sulzer Type 2 diesels, and Type 2s began pair-workings between Glasgow and Aberdeen with the 'down' "Granite City" and the 'up' "Bon Accord".

Class 55 'Deltic' No. D9000 *Royal Scots Grey,* seen at Waverley with the 11.00am to King's Cross on 17th April 1965.

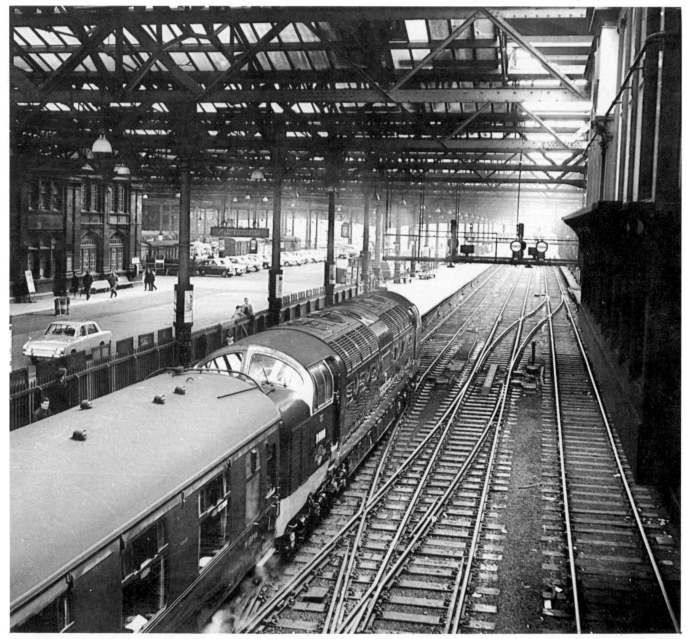

Platform 10 of Waverley Station, on 18th April 1965, and 'Deltic' No. D9004 *Queen's Own Highlander* stands at the head of a 'down' train.

A train for Glasgow leaves Inverness Station on 3rd April 1965 powered by a pair of Birmingham RCW/Sulzer Type 2 diesels.

Beattock Station, in March 1965, as English Electric Type 4 diesel No. D295 enters with an 'up' Glasgow to Liverpool express.

A three-car diesel multiple unit leaves platform 4 of Princes St. Station, Edinburgh on the afternoon of 8th May 1965.